# HVAC BUSINESS GUIDE MADE SIMPLE

I was born in Sunbury, Pennsylvania, where I lived until my parents separated. When I was five years old, my mother moved my three brothers and me to California. I was the third child and can remember to this day what it felt like to not have a father when I was growing up.  I also remember watching my mother struggle to feed three boys and herself.  We lived in homeless shelters, where we had to stand in line for a hot meal and wait for the doors to open at night so that we could have a place to sleep, only to be awakened at 6 in the morning because we had to leave. We never had enough in those years. And that is the ugly memories that stand out the most of being a child, well along with a screwed up abusive stepdad those memories too stand out, but this book is not about that, but my prayers go out to the people and families with these struggles.

When I turned 21, I met my soon wife to be, we had our first child, a boy. Later in life, we were homeless at times, and during those times when I looked at my son, I couldn't imagine putting him through what I had to experience as a child.  There's nothing like having a child to make you want to change your life. I focused on my situation and concluded that if I set my mind on a goal, I could accomplish anything. But I knew it would not be easy.  I had to change the way I thought, and I had to change patterns that had been with me for a lifetime. I tried different jobs.  I was a cashier, a jailer, a security guard, a cable installer and others. I learned things from every job I had. None of them seemed quite right.  Still, I was determined to find the right fit.  Then I found a job with an HVAC company and found a trade that seemed to suit me, and I felt my path was set.  I settled in and learned everything I could gain, and watched everything that everyone else did, and soaked up every bit of information that was available to me and worked hard to become very proficient. When I gained the confidence to step out on my own, I did so, thinking all the while that I could accomplish anything that I set my mind to achieve.  But I needed a plan. I was a good HVAC installer and service technician, and I had the feeling that this proficiency and knowledge would lead me down the road to success.  By that time, I was a young parent with a wife and three kids to support, and I had concluded that in order to have enough money to support my family, I needed to work for myself. With that in mind, I opened my business in 2011

The first year I had one employee, me and my wife. We worked out of our house and made enough money to pay the bills. I was doing ok the first year. By the second year, we were working out of our first building and had three more employees. Five years later we had fifteen employees and eleven service vehicles.

Owning your own company is not always easy. Sometimes you work all day and even when you're sleeping. Still, I pushed forward and little by little achieved my success. I followed my heart, marched forward to the drums, and didn't let anyone hold me back. I always looked for the lesson in any difficulties and learned along the way.  It has been said that when you follow what you were born to do that doors open for you and it's true. People appeared to help me, doors opened, where there were none, I learned what I needed to learn, continually educated myself, and continued to move forward. This book is part of that journey thus far.  I hope it inspires you to live your dream.

# TABLE OF CONTENTS


1.  The Dream

2.  forming the business

3.  Cultivating a Client Base

4.  Business Manners

5.  Staying Motivated

6.  Business Operation: *How to Stay Focused and Organized Through Growth*

7.  The Sales Process

8.  The Service Call Process

9.  Creating the Estimate

10. Resources

*the dream*

For most people, starting their own business is scary. There are many reasons for this, none of which matter except for the fact that they can keep you from realizing your dream can come to life. Thoughts like *where do I start?* Or *where will I get the money to start my business?* Or *how will I pay the bills and support my family?* Come to mind. These are all legitimate questions and concerns.        We live in a world that's always changing, and some, jobs are difficult to find and even more difficult to keep.  If you have such concerns, then hold the job you have while moving forward in life you want to be patient but persistent. There are other avenues available to take.

While this manual is written primarily for the HVAC individuals who want to go out on his own, it is also written for those who already have an HVAC business and want to learn more.  There is a multitude of resources online.  Find them.  Many cities and states have adult education programs for HVAC technicians. The Government offers Grants for those looking to acquire a skill.

- If you have good credit, you may qualify for a line of credit that will enable you to keep your current job while accumulating equipment and getting a client base for your new business.

- If neither of these work for you, then you need to take baby steps. Work your current job, while always moving forward into your new business by whatever means available, reading technical books on the field of HVAC, or learning new methods from those around you.

There is always a way to make your dreams come true.  Find it.

The most important qualities to have in any endeavor are those of faith, determination, and absolute self-confidence.  You must keep your eye on your goal and never waiver.  This is the secret to success.  In that, however, may have the temptation to take shortcuts or to behave unethically in your desire to get ahead.  This is an enormous mistake.  In all aspects of life, you must act with absolute integrity.

You be able to wake up every morning knowing that you have nothing to hide, and ready to give your best.  You must go to sleep every night knowing that you gave it you're all in thought word and deed.  You must be able to look your customers in the eyes with absolute honesty. There are no secrets in the world.  All things come to light eventually, and there's nothing worse than seeing the look of betrayal in a customer's eye. Trust is something that can never be recovered.  Equally important is the fact that living too far into the future promotes anxiety and remembering too far into the past promotes depression.  Now is the only moment when you can live your life, make changes, and forge ahead.

After confidence and determination come the stage of thoughtful planning and living into your dream. This stage is paramount to your success. What does your business look like to you?  What kind of clientele do you wish to attract? How much money do you want to make the first year?  How do you want to grow your business?  Most importantly, what will be owning your own business feel like and what can you do right now to set foot on the path that will lead you to have your own HVAC business? What can you do right now? This is the attitude you must assume,
To continue success.

# Chapter 2 forming your business

You need to research the regulations required to obtain your license? Do you need to investigate codes that govern the installation of HVAC systems? Do you need to establish a budget consisting of your living expenses vs. cash flow? How can you make this work? Then decide to take at least one step every day toward your goal. Stay focused and committed. If you need to forego some of the luxuries of your life at this moment, to create a better future, do so. Such sacrifices will be only temporary. It is important to remain dedicated and to have the self- discipline to proceed regardless of any challenge's life throws in your path. The moment you are ready to quit is usually the moment miracles occur. Andrew Carnegie is an inspiration that went from rags to riches a poor boy that rose to the top to be one of the richest men in history, I encourage you to read his story. It's inspiring.

Starting a business, it is clear that you will need and want to step up your bookkeeping. If you do not have a computer and can afford one, purchase one with a spreadsheet and database program. Sales on computers happen all the time, look for them. If you cannot afford a computer with a spreadsheet application, hire a bookkeeper in the beginning. This will save you time and money. Trust me I know.

After you place your business plan on paper, you will need to move forward with obtaining the proper documentation that shows that you are who you say you are and that you can do what you say you can do. Those who are stepping out to create their own business will need the following:

- Trade license

- City Business licenses, IRS EIN #

- Articles of Incorporation

- Insurances

Make a list of those items required that you have not fulfilled and set a date by which you will have your trade license making sure well in advance that you have met all the requirements.  If the time isn't fixed, it doesn't exist. Remember, step by step and be sure to stop and see what you've accomplished. Little by little, you can do it!

*cultivating a client base*

Now that you have set your goal, fulfilled your requirements, written your business plan and obtained the required licenses, insurance, and state and federal tax numbers, you will want to cultivate your client base. In executing this significant step, keep a record of the direction from where your leads are coming.

In the HVAC business leads can come from any direction, and each lead is as important as another.  Get your pen out and write them down.  If possible, and even in the early stages, work out a marketing budget as part of your overhead cost which is usually 5% of your revenue, realizing that in the beginning when you are building your base a lot of your marketing will be spread out, the fact that *you are in business* to the appropriate potential clientele.  Possible avenues of marketing include:

- Word of mouth – positives reviews by word of mouth are the result of developing a good reputation based on excellent workmanship.

- Flyers: create a small brochure outlining the services you offer and spend a Sunday putting them on mailboxes or putting them on windshields at the mall. Your flier should have the name of your company and the services you provide with a contact number or email. You can use this method for running specials. Note do not put them in the mailbox, but on the side, it is illegal to open a someone's mailbox other than yours.

- Direct Mail – this is one of the most effective ways of getting your name into the public eye.  A 2000 to 5000 amount of mail postcards with a good mailing list which can be downloaded immediately into your database is a great way to get your name into the public because even one response for service or installation can pay for the entire campaign.  Many sites provide mailing lists for specific targets. If you have a computer, you can generate postcards – the least expensive way to reach your target clientele. Alternately, a reasonable Quick Print Company can provide post cards and business cards. You may also use this method to run specials. Vista print is a company that works well.

- Having a presence on the internet is essential as well. Google AdWords and Google Places, allows you to list your business and pay per click.  You can develop your own web page and upload it or have someone whose business is to create web-pages for companies to do it for you. There are quite a few so be prepared to surf the internet until you find the site that suits you.

- Email marketing has also proven to be successful in many cases. Lists Again, the name of your company, contact information (reply or click email) what you offer and specials if any.

- Social media sites like Facebook and LinkedIn are also good sources because you want a potential customer to find you regardless of what avenue they choose.

- List your name in the phone book white and yellow pages which is also online. But I warn you on this with new technology like smartphones, I prefer to use my money online mostly, only use a small budget in phone books if any.

- Lead generating companies like Home Advisor, and Home Warranty Companies angies list are good leads as well.

- Call the Construction Industries Division in your city and make a list of new General Contractors. Call them and arrange to meet with them this also helps.

It is essential always to be marketing your business. The increased business allows you to grow exponentially. To achieve this goal, you must invest what you've made into your future growth even if it means you must forego Cable TV or to eat out for a few months.  Always pay attention to the marketing avenue that brings the most responses. This will save time and energy. Remember, word of mouth is the best, most cost effective marketing you can have.  One excellent job with the right customer will bring you hundreds more.

*business manners*

Equal in providing excellent technical and mechanical service is providing exceptional customer service. Customer service and professional service go hand in hand. In addition to marketing, making a good first impression and ensuring customer satisfaction is paramount to building your business. You never could make a good first impression more than once, and a wrong first impression remains in the mind of the customer forever.

How many times have you heard the comment, *the customer is always right?* Well, it's true. Ask yourself this: *Is the customer right to expect expert service? Are they right to expect that whatever problem they have with their HVAC will be resolved in a courteous, professional manner at a reasonable price?* I would say that the answer to both questions is yes. What would you say? What would you expect if you were in their position? Bring the attitude of excellent service to your business and to your life, and you will be rewarded greatly. There will be times when patients will be required. Times when you have an issue and need to figure out how your work will proceed. You will need to be armed with a straightforward manner and the facts to support you – proper codes, or the appropriate way in which to proceed with a problematic installation and repair to get it resolved. Do not become defensive or argumentative. Keep your voice pleasant and low, and overcome the discussion with the facts. Because you know your business, it is easy, with mindfulness and a friendly demeanor, to win your customer over with the points. For example, A repair is more effective if done this way instead of another way.

We can repair this unit, but it will cost you more in the long run because you may have to rebuild it often . . . And so forth.  This kind of demeanor ensures that one great review by word of mouth and consistent and excellent work can turn into hundreds of satisfied customers. Remember always to maintain a calm voice.


 Excellent customer service begins with the first call or email.  If a phone call comes in, answer with your business name followed by your name. For example: it's a great day at *"R T Heating, Cooling, and Plumbing, Angelo speaking, how may I help you"* This is the perfect response to a customer's first phone call because you have let the customer know that they have reached the correct number and you are waiting to fulfill their HVAC needs and were having a great day maybe we can help them have a great day. It provides an opening for them to clearly express their problem and have some comfort. Some people do not communicate well on the phone.  Give them a chance to speak, empathize with their problem *"oh my goodness, you must be frantic (worried, upset, hot, cold) we need to fix that right away."* I always like to use 'sir' and 'ma'am' until I know their name.  Then I use Mr. or Mrs. or Ms unless they ask me to use their given name, Nancy, Bob and so forth.  Formality is good manners.  It shows that you respect your customers. If they fail to identify themselves, you *"May I ask to whom I am speaking?"*.  In this way, you can guide the conversation to get the information you need such as the age of equipment location type forced air or radiant heat are, they a member or have they worked with us before, *"Mrs. Brown, I have 11 and 3 open tomorrow for service. Would that work for you?"* Try to accommodate your customer as best you can.  They will remember that you made your best effort.  The same courtesy applies to any email responses.  If possible, always have someone answer the phone in person.  A missed call – even if you have voice messaging - is a missed opportunity to make a sale or schedule a service call.  If you have someone who doubles as a receptionist/bookkeeper, you can forward calls to a cell phone, or if they are doing errands, you can send the office phone calls to your cell. It is your customers who are the lifeblood of your business. It is so easy to be pleasant, Courtesy and good manners go a long way in establishing the relationship you will have with your customer.

        Follow up with your scheduled service call. Arrive on time.  If you're early, people will think you're over-anxious. If you're late, they will think you don't care. My company usually gives a 2-hour window in which we will arrive and a call when on the way.  Either way, have the customer's phone number and call them to tell you will be coming either earlier than expected or a bit later. If it's earlier. Ask them if you can begin the work earlier. If it's more later, ask them the same question.  Either way – if the time frame is moderate, their answer will be yes, come by.  Your work clothes should be free of stains and your personal hygiene unquestionable.  There should be no smoking, no food present while on the job trash laying around, etc.  Have all the tools you will need with you.  Bring shoe covers if that's your protocol.  Always greet the customer at the door with *"Hello, Mrs. Brown, I'm Angelo with R T heating cooling and plumbing here to fix your furnace."*  Again, respect and manners combined with excellent service – technical expertise - go a long way to keeping your customer happy.

 Once you troubleshoot the system, take the time to explain the problem and the options available carefully. If they need an estimate, make sure you have an email, FAX phone or address to send it to.  If you can perform the evaluation on site all the better. If you can fix it but not warranty the work, make sure they know the reasons why and its stated-on paper.  If you can offer to finance, let them know and the small interest rate you will need to charge to carry them.  Make sure they put funds down equal to your labor cost and cost of material so that the only part of your financing is your profit.

Even under the best of circumstances, mistakes do occur. Be ready to admit fault and - if they have already paid for the repair - remedy the problem at no cost to the customer and learn to be more conscientious in the future. Your best-learned lessons are ones that cost you. Hopefully, you only make such mistakes once.

If for whatever reason, the repair is the result of no fault of yours, hopefully, you have either already told your customer the first time that the fix is not guaranteed or explained to them that such a repair is different from the original problem. If you have done so, then you have covered yourself honorably.  If it is a separate issue entirely, there should be no problem with initiating a *different* repair of the same unit. Remember if it is stated on paper it exists.

When recommending replacement, check all components to ensure everything that needs to be replaced. It is so important to act with transparency and integrity, in all instances and to guarantee your work and your materials.  In all things it is paramount to behave ethically, to do what you say you will do, to be polite and respectful.  This philosophy will hold you in good stead.  What I found is that when I maintain this attitude, I am always rewarded.  I may lose a customer in one instance but will add two or three others, in another situation.

*staying motivated*

Thus far you have set your goal, fulfilled your requirements, written your business plan, obtained the proper licenses, insurance, and state and federal tax numbers and learned how to interact with your customer in more a polite and professional manner. Whew, that's a lot to have accomplished. Pat yourself on the back for a job well done.

Now, it is important to remember that when you begin to change your circumstances vertically, you are like a rocket ship taking off from the earth to head into the Universe.  Some rockets launch easily. Some sit on their launch pads, ready to go but never leave.  When a rocket starts from earth into space, it needs an enormous amount of fuel and powerful engines to fight the pull of gravity. Look at the people, situations, and circumstances around you. If you view your desire to achieve your dream as the fuel, then those who support you and your vision are your booster engines.  Alternately, those people, situations, and circumstances that are not supportive are the gravity you must overcome. Just stay away from negative energy. Surround yourself with positive energy, people

All businesses have their ebb and flow.  All companies have days when they are horrifically busy and days when they are not.  This is the way of life.  At such times, it is essential to remain resolute. Learn from the times your business is slow and the times when it is so busy and ways to bridge the gap its called budgeting and planning sometimes you are working in your sleep trying to figure all this out. Do not allow doubts or fears to cloud your goals and what you wish to achieve – financial freedom, vacation, new car – all these are attainable and even though you feel as if you are moving two steps forward and one step back at times, you are still one step closer to your goal.

Write down what you have achieved thus far, and what you wish to accomplish. Sometimes you must revert back to baby steps until things begin to come your way again. Keep marketing, keep moving, keep pushing yourself forward step by step. Concentrate on little things that will make you move forward. Purchase a pin-up board and make it your dream list filled with things you want to see or do or buy. This will merely remind you of your dream and keep you motivated. You cannot do everything at once, so each day do one thing to complete one small goal to get to a big target. Perhaps you want to become EPA certified. How you will work toward your EPA certification.

There is something called a sun diagram, it goes like this draw a circle and put lines on the outer loop like rays from the sun On the sun's rays, list the steps that must be taken to achieve your goal with the goal itself in the center of the sun and the date by which it will be completed.  Begin by researching what steps to take to achieve that certification or goal which the small steps will be listed on the outer lines the sun rays.  As you complete each small goal, give yourself a pat on the back and do something nice for yourself. Once you have reached your primary goal in the center of the sun, reward yourself with something you've always wanted a big reward.

Too many times we become comfortable with the status quo – sitting on the couch watching television when we should be soaking up this world and everything in it.  A life well lived is a world explored.  Educate your mind, plan your future.  As is said, "A journey of a thousand miles begins with one step."  Take that step!  Use your time and energy to move forward in all things. Regardless of your religious beliefs, it is true that God helps those who help others.  So, don't forget about people along the way the world rewards those for taking risks to move forward in life.  Believe in yourself.  Move forward with faith, honesty, and integrity.  Opportunities come when you least expect them, and from directions, you might not have ever dreamed of. Also, there are so many books and courses to study, remember knowledge is limitless unless you make that way.

## CHAPTER 6

*Business operation - staying focused and organized through continued growth*

Keeping your focus on the work that is required to grow your business is paramount though sometimes tricky.  as they say "life happens and some of that life may have everything to do with you but nothing to do with the task at hand. This situation is equally applicable to large and small issues. If you are fortunate to have a family (wife or husband and children) who is supportive of you, you will need to learn how to balance both. Otherwise, you will turn around 10 years from now and have either a very successful business but a fragmented family or a good family relationship but a mediocre business.

You need not to choose one or the other but to balance both.  The issue is organizing, timing and the delegation of time and the tasks required. For many business owners, Sundays are sacred. They either take no calls and that day is devoted to their family, or they have one employee who is trustworthy to take emergency calls. These are situations you will need to work into.  Perhaps in the early days, you can take your spouse and children to deliver flyers and then eat dinner.  If your children are computer savvy, they can start the process of creating brochures or postcards.  Include your spouse and children when appropriate, and they will feel as if they are part of the process. Bookkeeping is relatively easy to learn, perhaps your spouse can take a continuing education course and learn to create spreadsheets and cost analysis proposals.  If you can include your family, there will be less pressure on you to carry the total weight.  By the same token, there will be times when you are engaged with the customer either in person or on the telephone when both family and employee should respect that moment. During such times, you may very well wish to do one of several things:

- If a customer call comes in and you are unable to take the call, either allow it to go to voicemail and return the call right away or answer the call and let the customer know that you will call them back within the hour then do so.  If their issue is of an emergency nature, try to be flexible and address their needs in whatever manner is possible.

- Employees need to know that if you are working on an estimate and your office door is closed, or you are on the phone that they are not to disturb you in any way. This rule needs to be set out right away with each employee. It will save time and annoyance in the long run. It is so easy to say, "Unless you are on fire, send me a message."  Any techs you may employ should, for the most part, know their trade. The nature of messaging by email and text makes communication much less invasive. This allows you, as the owner, to have hands-on experience with all bids without being interrupted and to only address as needed their concerns.

- At all times, you may wish to remember your excellent customer service rules.

- If you are the owner, salesperson, and technician, you have the luxury of deciding your schedule and priorities. You are responsible only for your own actions.  Working with employees is different. It is essential to be sensitive to their needs while getting the job done. Many owners have a Monday meeting in the morning before work begins.  At these meetings, employees are invited and encouraged to voice any concerns or complaints, as well as to discuss jobs that lie ahead.  Many times, employees may have ideas that improve service.  Don't be too quick to dismiss them. They may save you time and money.  It is essential to maintain as much of a standard protocol and routine as possible, adding additional positions and delegating as appropriate as you grow. Remember, very few problems signal the end of the world. All things can be reconciled.

- you will hope to have others participate in your company as it grows. Most notably would be:
  - The owner holds the ultimate decision-making process over all others in management. A good owner always works as hard, or harder, than his employees in ways they would never know of.  The owner will work with all General and Commercial Contractors concerning new construction or remodels or renovations.
  - The Operations Manager oversees the basic operations of the company including who is working and who is not, troubleshooting within the organization on all levels. It is the Operations Manager that sets the tone for how smoothly the business runs. The Operations Manager oversees scheduling service and installation calls and is also instrumental in keeping up on trends and advances in HVAC and can bring them to the attention of the owner, conducts sales of service and systems when possible. The Operations Manager should review all bills for materials from suppliers, investigate the possibility of quantity discounts from suppliers when possible. Can oversee implementing marketing and advertising under the supervision of the Owner. Can

interact with customers as appropriate. He may be the person who works up all domestic bids or Commercial bids before the Owner reviews.

- o The Field Supervisor oversees individual projects, works with the Operations Manager on scheduling, quality control, and emergency management. Scheduling programs should be networked with all other office computers.

- o The Office Manager oversees all paper involved with the running of the business. The Office Manager may or may not be the receptionist and dispatcher, bookkeeper, supervise the issuing of payroll, ensuring that all payroll, sales tax, state and federal taxes are paid in a timely manner, conduct client billing, pay all bills associated with running the business, makes sure that all licenses are current and give notice when continuing education is required. Depending on the size of your business you may need separate dispatchers and customer service reps.

As you grow, these categories may divide. You may have split off the job of estimations and bids and create a new position. The office manager may need someone to answer the phone and dispatch techs for the day. These things will settle themselves as you grow. All employees should be thoroughly vetted when necessary. Check references. Do they have the qualifications they claim to have? In addition to technical experience, and where the operations are concerned, look for experience in marketing, bookkeeping, business administration. Some owners require that their employees bond themselves. That's a decision you'll have to make when you come to it. All this knowledge comes as you grow. Just be aware of what's possible and what you need to run a successful business.

## *sales process with case studies*

Many of the same principals apply to both the sales and service process. The sales process begins as soon as the customer contacts the office staff which, in most cases, will be the receptionist. Whoever answers the phone has the first contact with the customer the first person to provide service and an opportunity to offer other products or services to your customer.  A call for repairs on a forced air furnace can turn into a furnace and or refrigerated air installation.  As discussed, she or he should be polite and professional. It is the receptionist who will usually assess the need and direct the call to you, the Owner, the Operations Manager or salesman, who will either schedule, repair, service or performs a sales call depending upon whether someone is looking for a new furnace or AC unit, or just needs something repaired.

If someone is looking to purchase a new unit – heating or air – the sale person/ comfort advisor Operations Manager or Owner should take the call.  If the customer wants a new HVAC system to replace their existing system, the information that needs to be known is.

- What kind of system currently provides heat and air for the house?

- Does the customer want to replace the existing system or just repair?

Most of your customers will have no idea of the square footage of their home or the current system they may want to replace the system, so you will need to make a sales call. With that in mind, the salesman/comfort advisor can meet with the customer prepared with what is available for their existing unit AND information on options that are available. If the customer is participating in a renovation or remodel, then there may be many options. Units that provide hot water and radiant heat, for example, or individual units to cool bedrooms ductless systems. If possible, have a package ready with all relevant information on the services and units you provide.

In many cases, if you are replacing a forced air furnace, it is relatively easy to convince the client to go with refrigerated air. However, for the receptionist, and the Operations Manager or salesman/ comfort advisor, it is essential to assess the need first so that you can provide the information on the service required. New Residential or Commercial Construction installations should always be referred to you, the owner of the company. Or someone who is trained for these estimates. Remember to find a need so you can provide a solution. When it comes to sales

- CASE STUDY: It's 98 degrees and noon when a call comes in concerning a forced air unit that is not blowing any air. Keeping in mind the protocol from chapter 4, the receptionist takes the call and pulls up the schedule, informing the caller that a technician can be at the residence between 2 and 4. The receptionist immediately takes the address and phone number and then ask the age and brand of the system is told by the customer that the unit is old, has been repaired many times, that it should be replaced, and that she has no idea of the brand. The receptionist asks how the customer came to call and is told the number was obtained from the Yellow pages. Receptionist generates the work order and informs the comfort advisor Operations Manager that he has a sales call in 2 hours. This gives him the time to prepare a package of options for the customer. Let us review the process:
  - the receptionist takes customer phone call according to the protocol in chapter 4

  - Assesses need and responds accordingly
  - Notates address and phone
  - Establishes time of the service call
  - Completes work order with requirements and sends to Operations Manager or Salesman/ comfort advisor
  - Operations manager or Salesman has time to gather sales information based on need and/or anticipated need before making the Service Call.
  - Checklist – name, address, phone, work order, information on replacement systems and information on available systems (air filtration, air conditioning systems) that might make them more comfortable.  Be prepared to show the customer how any system you install works and can make their lives easier or more comfortable at a reasonable cost.

## *service call procedure*

Once the Service Call procedure has been established and executed, will make the service call. Although we have addressed some of these steps in the chapter on customer service, the perfect service call would look something like this:

(1) Do not park in the driveway. You may drip oil on the pavement (2) Make sure trash does not fall out of your vehicle. (3) Be prepared with your notepad and the proper tools for the job (4) Do not ring the doorbell a family member might be sleeping knock first before you ring the doorbell then call and email if necessary, call dispatch and wait 15 minutes. (5) Don't look in windows keep a proper distance from the door. (6) have shoe covers ready and a floor mat to put your shoe covers on this will also show the customer you care. (7) Customer answers the door present your name and company they invite you in. Shoe covers are on you ask what brings us out here today. (8) Ask where the appliance is located and explain again about the company's service charge. before you fix anything, you will get an authorized approval signature. (9) Once you found the repair and verified with the office if its warranty or not. You will gather your pricing from your flat rate pricing guide and present it to the customer Mr or Mrs do you have a minute, always show sympathy explain what you found how you can help. Present your price, if there a service member then they get a discount 10 to 15% if not offer them a membership and apply the discount.(10) maybe the system is old and needs to be replaced instead of repaired usually over 10 years of age you should explain current and future cost of repairs on an older system is not recommended for repair but it always up to the customer we only provide a menu.(11) Always keep your cool if you need to call the office or a supervisor step outside or go to your vehicle be confident if you need help call someone tech support if necessary.(12) Remember to get everything in writing and

never to leave angry call a manager before you drive away and explain the situation if any arises.(13) If all went well close out the call get your signatures required leave brochures on indoor air quality and remind them of any other service you offer. Don't forget the check or the boss might be upset.

***creating the estimate, closing the sale***

A good comfort advisor should be doing nothing but giving someone what they already want or need a menu to let them choose from. Whether it's a service call for a repair or a new installation, you are always providing the customer with a service or a unit that they want or need but provide multiple options.  You may offer them a choice of which they were unaware of, in a neutral manner, they will either accept or decline remember it is our job to find the needs and the concerns they have then show them solutions. If they agree, great, if they refuse, its ok the faster this takes place, the quicker you can move on to a new client, but please don't rush. If you give them what they want in an efficient, professional manner, they will be your client forever which means that a 'no' today may mean a 'yes' tomorrow.

Regardless of their budget, when your assessment has been done, you will need to study the evaluation and come up with the most cost-effective, budget effective solution possible considering the following:

- Did the existing unit meet their needs?

- Was its reasonably trouble free for the extent of its life?

- Taking inflation into account, what would the cost be of replacing the existing system with a comparable one?

- Given the following elements, the following formula is acceptable for estimating a replacement unit:

    - Example Labor for tech and helper $25+$12= 37.  Per hour

Hours per day to install 8 hrs.

Days to install 3 days

Total $37 x 8 x 3 = $888

 Equipment plus material cost $5500


Total $6388.00

Divide the total of labor and the unit cost by .5 = $12776.00

This is a divisor method you start with 100 % look at your overhead on your P&L  profit and loss statement which may be 30% add 20% for the profit you want to make added together which will then be = 50% then subtract 50 from 100% = 50 your divisor is .50 or .5  This will help with your Total estimate for replacing existing equipment. Note the divisor can change depending on overhead or your wanted profit. This covers your overhead and should leave you with a net profit after taxes. Note only suggestions overhead should be under 30% equipment purchased should not more 45% on P&L advertisement 5% try to keep these numbers low as possible, but the advertisement is just 5% in my opinion.

- Have ready an additional estimate for other units in their price range and their advantages over the comparable unit.  You should also have estimates for additional equipment they might want – humidifier, water softener system, air purification system, include tax in all estimates, so it isn't a shock. Don't provide too many estimates because people shut down if they have too many choices 3-5 options is good. Nevertheless, be able to address their concerns.

Make an appointment to present the estimates and answer any questions they might have. Offer your additional suggestions and explain why you have given these separate bids and what other equipment you have to offer them as in comfort or saving money on utilities. From the time you present the estimates, it is a simple matter of allowing them to decide. If money is a problem, remind them that you offer to finance at a reasonable rate. Ask them if they need some time to decide, if not, write up the order.

- Remember:
    - Know your merchandise – you are the pro, know your job.
    - If you know your merchandise and job, you will exude an air of true confidence.

- o Do not be too formal or familiar – build a friendly relationship based on mutual trust and respect.  Addressing them as Mr. and Mrs. until they say otherwise is a sign of respect and good manners.

- o Listen to their concerns.  They are spending a lot of money with you.

**Sample Estimate**

Company Name

**Customer
Information**


**We propose to install a Trane 80.000 BTU up flow 17-inch-wide s9v2 high-efficiency furnace with a 3 ton 18 seer condenser with a coil. A lyric Wi-Fi thermostat is included. All parts and labor are covered for completion. All work will be performed in a proper workmanship manner and done according to local codes.**
**Cost $11.989**
**Tax $839.23**
**Total $12.828.23**
**We provide a three-year labor warranty on work, 1yr service contract Trane 10 yr parts warranty.**
***note A surge protector for ac will be provided.**
If you accept this proposal, please contact our office for scheduling.
upon signing return via email or by mail. All work will be provided in a proper workmanship manner.
We will pull all permits required; an inspector will inspect the work following the completion of work.
This proposal shall expire in ninety (90) days from this date.
Company policy requires 50% down and remaining balance due upon completion.
Any cancelations will result in a 20% restocking fee

.



Sincerely,
**Your Name**

Customer signature upon acceptance:

CHAPTER 10

*promoting teamwork*

Very few people are successful in business by themselves. It takes a good team to create your vision.  From the first customer call to the man who cleans your building at the end of the day, all the people in your life have a role to play.  If you are fortunate, you will have a team around you that compliments you and each other. At the same time, and despite the similarities, everyone is different. So, while there is a protocol of expected professional behavior in your business structure (be on time, look your best, within that protocol are individual personalities.

Everyone that you work with will have their own problems, their own struggles. They are worthy of respect. At the same time, you, as an owner, are ultimately responsible for who you hire and what they bring with them to your company. Checking references is the best way to discover a potential employee's history and demeanor including background checks. Were they late all the time? Sick? Did they complain? More than that is trusting your own intuition about a person. Eventually, if you interview enough people, you will know instantly who will be a good fit and who will not.

That said, everyone has a bad day. Everyone goes through the crisis on occasion. On those infrequent occasions, it is essential to act with empathy and compassion, address the issue, and help where needed.  If you have built a good team, all members of your team will be willing, to cover for each other on those rare occasions when something goes wrong, they will all pull together to pick up the slack. The critical issue is to gather a team willing to accept other differences and work together and find their qualities in one another.

If you've read this book, you have a good start in creating a career for yourself in the HVAC world. Good luck with your dream! Note, please talk with an advisor, bookkeeper, etc we are not responsible for your business actions or financial improvement or outcome note that this book only explains experience that may help or may be relevant to the info you are looking for. Thank you for reading have a blessed life.

Sincerely Angelo Marti.

Resources

## technician job responsibilities are as followed.

- Be able to properly diagnose HVAC equipment.  ductless a/c units, split systems forced air furnaces, packaged a/c roof top units' hydronic boilers. Residential and light commercial.
- Be able to lift 50 lbs.
- Own and be able to use the proper HVAC equipment and tools electrical meter, monometer, gas leak detector, freon leak detector, refrigerant scale, necessary hand tools, refrigerant recovery machine. c/o combustion analyzer. Note* some equipment may be signed out for use but needs to be discussed with supervisor upon hire, but tools of the trade is always necessary for a tech to own for his or her work duties.
- Perform 4 to 5 HVAC service diagnostic calls per day.
- Communicate with office staff and customers regarding necessary repairs reschedules, return visits equipment, orders and warranty returns.
- Fill out proper work orders and time cards, collect all payments credit card, checks and cash. Also be able to use software and tablet.
- Explain service programs and repair cost to custom.

- Report all necessary to inform problems to supervisor or office.
- Work well with other employees with a team attitude mutual respect.

- Report to all necessary company meetings and be on time always.

- Be able and willing to train and help where necessary in HVAC areas of the trade.
- Turn in all receipts for gas and parts etc.
- Be responsible for work van cleanliness, scheduled oil changes through company and be responsible for company borrowed tools.
- Maintain a positive attitude with fellow coworkers and customers.
- Provide an active driver license high school diploma and be able to be insured. necessary relevant work experience 2-5 years.

## Understanding your billable hour is vital to business it's what you need to charge hourly.

So let's say you pay your tech 25 dollar an hour remember general liability and workers compensation insurance and all expenses we need to re-coop it somewhere all those overhead expenses it is said that your techs are only 50 to 60 % billable that's because they are traveling back and forth job to job or supply houses and no one is paying for that unapplied time but you. Now let's say he or she works 40 hours a week $25 x 40 = $1000 x 52 weeks which =$52,000 that's what you're paying out of pocket. However, remember if were only billing 50 % of the time that means we're just getting $26,000 worth of hard work out of the employee, he or she might be doing other things like driving back and forth from calls. So, we need to make up for the additional $26,000 plus we want a profit, remember we have other expenses don't forget the rent gas utilities etc. standard expenses is usually 30% percent of sales according to industry reports but may vary for each company, 30% is what you should be close too. So, if you were off to do $100,000 - $300,000 in sales, then 30% would be around $30,000 through $90,000 in overhead expenses. So, remember if were only billing 50 % of the time, we need to collect the other 50% making up for it on each call for each hour charged including expenses, so our $52,000 in employee annually pay plus let's say $47,624 in overhead expenses gives us a total of $99,00624 plus a 20% profit = $1824,530 then divided by 52 weeks = $2394.80 then divided by 40 hours = $59.287 because we only collect 50% of the time then $59.287 multiplied by 2 = $119.74 an hour. $119.74 an hour multiplied by 40 hours a week =$4789.60 multiplied by 52 = $249,059.90 that's if we bill each hour 8 hours a day but if we only bill 4 hours because of lost time, its = $124,529.50 if we get more hours billed then great if not our lost time is still charged for.  Remember the other formula used when bidding installs it be is done a little different vs. hourly service work. Here is another Example of your billable hour, let's say you have two employees at $25 an hour each x 2 = $50 an hour x 40 hours a week = $2000 x 52 weeks = $104,000 a year If we were doing  $200,000 to $500,000 in sales 30% of that would be $60,000 to $150,000 in overhead expenses, $104,000 for pay + $150,000  for expenses = $254,000 + 20% $63,500 = $317,500 then divided by 52 weeks =$6105 divided by 40 hours = $152.64 an hour x 2 for the other 50% = $305.28 an hour x 40 hours = $12,211.20 x 52 weeks = $634,982.40 for the year because we're only billing half the time because of lost time this would be $317,491.20, and this is why most company's go flat rate pricing which means  they have one flat fee including the repair which the hourly rate is built in so you don't really show that. However, this has its advantages you don't bill more if the job takes longer and you don't bill less, so it's a balance at the end of the year. I highly recommend flat rate and of course your billable hour could be in the middle or lower it depends on how much revenue you're doing plus your sales. Remember to get your profit and loss statement and get your overhead expenses off that, or you can try to project your upcoming annual sales and go off of that.

Hello, my name is Angelo Marti, and I am a successful HVAC contractor. An example that you can become who you want to be in life with a little hard work. I founded my company when I was 28 after a life of hardship and struggle. I began with inspiration and determination and watched my life unfold becoming successful in the first year. This was no accident. My company took off because of the way I formed it and the way I ran it. Now, I want to share my formula with you. This book will show you step-by-step how to become a professional HVAC contractor or salesperson, so if you're looking for a change, this is it.